The Art of
RUG
HOOKING

The Art of
RUG
HOOKING

Anne D. Mather

Sterling Publishing Co., Inc. New York

Photographer: Ron Lindahn, Valhalla Studio, Rabun Gap, Georgia
Artist: Tom Mather
Designer: Deborah Dutton
Editor: Claire Bazinet

Library of Congress Cataloguing in Publication
Mather, Anne D.
The art of rug hooking / Anne D. Mather.
p.   cm.
Includes index.
ISBN 0-8069-1763-6 (hc)
1. Rugs, Hooked. 2. Rugs, Hooked—Patterns. I. Title.
TT850.M39   1998
746.7'4—dc21   98-28321
                                                                  CIP

1   3   5   7   9   10   8   6   4   2

First paperback edition published in 1999 by
Sterling Publishing Company, Inc.
387 Park Avenue South, New York, N.Y. 10016
© 1998 by Anne D. Mather
Distributed in Canada by Sterling Publishing
% Canadian Manda Group, One Atlantic Avenue, Suite 105
Toronto, Ontario, Canada M6K 3E7
Distributed in Great Britain and Europe by Cassell PLC
Wellington House, 125 Strand, London WC2R 0BB, England
Distributed in Australia by Capricorn Link (Australia) Pty Ltd.
P.O. Box 6651, Baulkham Hills, Business Centre, NSW 2153, Australia
Printed in China

Sterling ISBN 0-8069-1763-6 Trade
0-8069-1801-2 Paper

To Mary Williamson
and in memory of
Naomi Stopher

Lucetta's Tree of Life. Hooked by Edie Gerver. Designed by Pearl K. McGown.
Size: 57 by 85 inches. This rug took first place in a North Carolina State Fair competition and
"Best of Show" at a National Guild of Pearl K. McGown Hookrafters Show held in St. Louis.

Contents

Art in a Rug

Endearing, Inspiring

Antique Fruit Basket. Hooked by Martha Morris. An adaptation of a 19th-century theorem painting, designed by Martha Morris for Lib Callaway. Size: 25 by 35 inches

Ours is an old craft.
Our ancestors hooked rugs
For floors, of course,
But also
For walls, to keep out wind,
For beds, to warm the feet.

Old, untitled rug. From the collection of Anne Mather. Size: 42 by 66 inches

Old rugs are not as perfect as ours.
A hooker ran out of color for a rose or
   background
So she finished it with another—
Often one that didn't quite match or
   blend.
People call this primitive or naive.
But it is what is missing from perfection.
It is art.

Rose Bird. Hooked by Anne Mather. Designed by Patsy Becker. Size: 24 by 34 inches

Hookers meet, like quilters,
In each other's homes,
In old church halls.

A local teacher's flock grows, then retracts.
There may be ten women or five
Gathered around a wooden table
Like birds at a cozy nest,
Pulling strings of wool up
To feed their rugs.

Endearing Elegance. Hooked by Mary Williamson. An adaptation, by Pris Buttler, of an 18th-century watercolor-and-ink painting, "Two Women," circa 1815. Size: 29 by 32.5 inches

This is one of the craft's gifts,
"The endearing elegance of female friendship"
Samuel Johnson called it.

Blue Ridge Rug Camp. Hooked by Anne Mather. Adapted by Robin Hasty and Jeanette Szatkowski from a pen-and-ink sketch of Valle Crucis Conference Center. From the collection of Katherine and Charles Lord. Size: 22 by 29.5 inches

Though ancient, ours is a little known craft.
Most must travel to learn it.
Thus we pilgrim to rug camps—
Weeklong workshops held on a mountain top in Tennessee
A one-hundred-year-old retreat center in North Carolina
An old monastery in South Dakota.
Humble sites
The sorts of places that won't mind—might actually welcome—
A few dozen women with a very messy habit:
Lint everywhere
Long hours
Loud laughter.

High Tea. Hooked by Betty Morning. Designed by Jane McGown Flynn. Size: 24 by 36 inches

At camp
Student and teacher meet
Perhaps for the first time.
But they are not strangers.

For rug hooking is an older
  woman's art form
And thus permeated
With the bread-and-butter notes
Of another age.

Warm letters,
Photos,
Odd creative yearnings:
These have been shared
For many months.

Three Little Kittens. Hooked and adapted by Anne Mather. Inspired by an image from the animated film
"The Tail of Samuel Whiskers" from The World of Peter Rabbit and Friends® animated series.
Copyright © Frederick Warne & Co., 1993. Size: 28 by 36 inches

Teachers take what they know
About each student
And dye it into colors for her rug.

This red resembles the roses in her garden.
This brown, a pet cat's fur.

Wrong Number. Hooked by Bryan Hancock. Adapted by Patsy Becker, from an 1800s pattern. Size: 26 by 41 inches

The first day of class is like Christmas:
Each woman opens her bag of many colors
Made just for her.

Two Houses Welcome. Hooked by Marguerite Culberson. Designed by Pearl McGown. Size: 19 by 37 inches

Each teacher also has a long table,
Swamped with dyed wools.
And garbage pails, overflowing with
Plaids and stripes,
Torn-up suits and camel-hair vests.
Reds and rusts,
Persimmons and purples.

And colors you recognize but cannot name:
Of fresh pine straw
And old tin roofs
And snow shadows.

Dancing Bears. Hooked by Anne Mather. Adapted, with permission, from GEAR's wallpaper design, American Country wallpaper book, Imperial Wallcoverings. Size: 15 by 33 inches

Students make field trips through this messiness,
Scrounging through the wool piles,
Triumphant
When, like bargain basement shoppers,
They find the perfect piece.
For in that wonderful, tumbleweed way
That creativity works,
The right colors for each rug
Always appear.

Plantation Fruits. Hooked by Judy Hill. Designed by Marion Ham. Size: 29.5 by 52 inches

Then the work begins.
To go to rug camp is to learn
What it means to apprentice under a master.
Teachers may hold court for twelve hours a day.
Silences become long and comfortable
As students bend over their rugs
Like monks over ancient manuscripts.

Nantucket Whaling. Hooked and designed by Beverly Goodrich. Size: 23 by 40 inches

Hooking begins with piles of burlap.
Like painters who say they do their best work
On newsprint, not canvas,
Hookers often work with this humble material.

Our ancestors hooked on feed sacks.
Bent, filed nails were their tools.

The Littlest Angel. Three variations. Top, hooked by Faith Kern and made into a pillow. Middle and bottom, by Anne Mather. Latter, from the collection of The Task Force for Child Survival and Development. Designed by Barbara Bancroft for Marion Ham. Size: 15.5 by 28 inches

Burlap stinks.
It has a faint, warm, wheaty smell
And it's rough to the touch.
It has flaws in it:
Thick little lumps
That worry and distract.

Portion of unfinished rug. *Abram's Creek Stag*. Hooked and designed by Bett McLean.
Full size: 53 by 53 inches

Burlap waiting to be hooked looks
Like a torn page
From a child's coloring book.
Patterns have outlines, simple lines,
That's all.
A rug pattern is but a sketch.
Hookers supply the rest.

Cats and Flowers. Hooked by Maryon Clonts. Adaptation, by Lib Callaway, of early pattern (circa 1810). Size: 24 by 52 inches

Some rug patterns are very old.
They have been hooked hundreds and
    thousands of times.

But new or old, rug patterns
Celebrate the familiar:
Fruit baskets,
Family pets

Down on the Farm. Hooked by Faith Kern. Designed by Patsy Becker. Size: 28 by 43 inches

Houses,
Flowers in abundance,
And farm animals—
Sheep, especially.

Annie's Dream. Hooked by Mary Lu Cole. Designed by Patsy Becker. Size: 40 by 63 inches

Patterns often have romantic names:
Annie's Dream
Ramona
New England Bouquet.

The Cottage Garden. Hooked by Anne Mather. Designed by Jeanne Benjamin, New Earth Designs.
Size: 16.5 by 20 inches

Rugs have borders
Scrolls, sometimes,
Or patterns borrowed from quilts:
Patchwork, log cabin
And clamshell
(which hookers call lamb's tongue).

Chicken Rug. Hooked by Mary Williamson. Adapted from a design by Emma Tennant. From the collection of Peggy and Eston Melton. Size: 24 by 40 inches

Or borders may evolve from the rug itself:
Waves on a sea pictorial,
Fences around flowers,
Barbed wire around barred fowl.

Woman Who Ran with the Wolf. Hooked and designed by Anne Mather. Size: 26 by 30 inches

Primitive rugs use wide-cut wool and
Little, if any, shading.
The outlines of a sketch are hooked in one color,
Filled in with another.
Primitive hookers delight in using "as is":
Plaids, checks, herringbones,
Garnered from pieces of used clothing
At garage sales and thrift shops.

Motherly Love. Hooked and designed by Bett McLean. Size: 24 by 36 inches

Primitive hooking is often abstract.
A string of orange suggests a sunset.
Five stitches become a bumble bee.

May Morris. Hooked by Mary Williamson. Adapted by Jane McGown Flynn from Pimpernel, a wallpaper design by William Morris.
Size: 33 by 68 inches

Tapestry rugs use finer cut wool:
Often as slight as embroidery floss.
Wool must be of very good quality
To be cut into such slim threads,
Not to ravel or twist.

Rug hookers know texture.
They like to feel fine wool
Slide through their fingers.
A merino, like silk, massages.

Epaminondas. Hooked and designed by Anne Mather. Adapted from a pen-and-ink drawing by Inez Hogan in the children's book, "Epaminondas and His Auntie" by Sara Cone Bryant. Size: 28.5 by 33 inches

Hookers know color.
Each rug is a play on colors,
Though they are often muted.

When a shade is too stark,
The hooker subdues it with dye.
Blue turns orange into rust, for example.

Father Christmas. Hooked by Naomi Stopher. Designed by Jane McGown Flynn.
Size: 16 by 20 inches. From the collection of the Rabun County Public Library.

If too dull
Overdyeing enlivens:
Chartreuse awakens navy blue,
Makes it the color of a starry night sky.

You Can't Have My Wool Sweater. Hooked and designed by Pris Buttler; sheep are adapted from a cross-stitch pattern.
Size: 31 by 50 inches

Yet each rug must have its poison.
The odd touch:
A lilac that lingers.
Orange, where a red was expected.

But a little poison,
Like perfume,
Goes a long way.

Patchwork Rug. Hooked by Anne Mather. Designed by Happy and Steve DiFranza. Size: 30 by 38 inches

You see colors in rugs you'd never otherwise see.
They are created in kitchens,
Casserole-dyed
In old porcelain pots
On old stoves or backyard grills.

Natural dyes yield rich surprises:
Cactus beetles make a dusky salmon,
Madder root an orange.
Mistakes often become new creations—
Colors no crayon box ever held.

Mrs. Vick on Horseback. Hooked by Mary Williamson. Adapted from wall mural in Nita Yuma Plantation, Vicksburg, Mississippi. Size: 28 by 34 inches. From the collection of Lee and Ken Burson.

Hookers know the hypnotic luxury
Of repeated stitches.
The slow, spreading warmth that happens
When beauty materializes
Where only wool and burlap existed
   moments before.

Goldie on a Linsey Woolsey. Hooked by Anne Mather. Adapted from illustration in old children's book, *12 Well Known Stories*, author and date unknown. Size: 19 by 28 inches

Hookers know stories.
They tell them at camps and meetings.
Sometimes the craft seems but a backdrop
    to this banter,
This reminiscing of ladies no longer young.
The stories are told so often
The storytellers know
Just when to pause for a laugh.

Lakeside Cabin. Hooked by Anne Mather. Designed by Kathy Morton. Size: 20 by 30 inches. From the collection of Carol Maxwell.

Hookers stitch what they know into
   their rugs
So the rugs tell stories too.

Janelle. Hooked by Barbara Moran. Designed by Jane McGown Flynn. Size: 24 by 40 inches. From the collection of Claire and JanPiet Karssiens.

The warm, down-to-earth nurse,
Raised in an Irish family in a French town,
Hooks rugs as colorful as her stories.
Her joy
Slips in between the loops,
Burrows into the burlap,
So that in the presence of one of her rugs
You feel the overwhelming urge to smile or laugh
Or simply be joyful.

Jolly Lions. Hooked by Mary Williamson. Adapted by Lib Callaway from 18th-century rug. Size: 30 by 54 inches.
From the collection of Lee and Ken Burson.

The seamstress delights in even stitches
Tidy edges
Finishing finesse.

Mini Ramona. Hooked by Anne Mather. Designed by Jeanette Szatkowski, Harry M. Fraser Company. Size: 23 by 35 inches

The writer
delights in discovering
the likenesses of the two art forms
she loves.

For both writing and hooking
celebrate color,
explore metaphors,
exalt details.
Each art has a rhetoric—
repetitions, juxtapositions, puns—
each, its own rhythm.

And each creation grows with
   letting go.
What isn't there is as important
   as what is,
Like the sinking, now out-of-sight
   bobbin
is as important, maybe more,
than the caught fish.
Like the pianist's fingers
arched for their fall into sound,
build passion
by holding back.

North American Noah's Art. Hooked and designed by Faith Kern. Size: 66 by 96 inches

Women hook their pain,
Lifetimes of it:
Cancers, Alzheimer's, strokes,
Deaths and divorces.
The burlap is their altar cloth.
It absorbs, transmutes, this pain.

Turkish Primitive. Hooked by Mary Lu Cole. Designed by Jane McGown Flynn. Size: 32 by 56 inches

Women also hook what they
    don't know.

A shy woman weaves in the
    flame orange
She will never wear.

A psychiatric nurse
Brings not what she knows—
Psychosis, sickness, war—
But the childlike wonder of a
    new world:
Color, needlework, creativity.

Her rugs are a baptism in beauty.
Her rooster's tail feathers burst
    into peacock colors.
Her orientals sing with Imari
    blues and Egyptian reds.

Her rugs are healthy, innocent
Alive.

Three Marans. Hooked by Anne Mather. Designed by Emma Tennant. Size: 24 by 36 inches

The art is in this knowing and not knowing.

Pleasant View. Two variations. Top, hooked by Barbara Moran. Bottom, Anne Mather.
Designed by Patsy Becker. Size: 26 by 38 inches

It is why the same pattern always makes
a different rug
Under different hands.

Soul Melody. Hooked and designed by Kathleen Russell. From the collection of Roy and Elizabeth Turner. Size: 24 by 36 inches. Photo: Henry Troup and John Corcoran, Sterling Commercial Photography, New Cumberland, Pennsylvania.

These are some things that
Rug hookers know.

Rug Hooking

A $\mathscr{P}$ RIMER, PROJECTS
AND PATTERNS

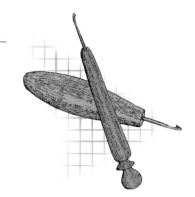

"We have come to think that duty should come first. I disagree. Duty should be a by-product...creative effort, the use of the imagination, should come first—at least for some part of every day of your life. It is a wonderful blessing if you will use it. You will become happier, more enlightened, alive, impassioned, lighthearted and generous to everybody else. Even your health will improve. Colds will disappear and all the other ailments of discouragement and boredom."

Brenda Ueland
***If You Want to Write: A Book about Art, Independence and Spirit*, 1938**

How to Hook

The women whose rugs are featured here are of varying ages, careers, and backgrounds (see Appendix). Most are total unknowns in the world of art, though a few are well-known in rug-hooking circles. Most of these women are my friends and neighbors in small communities in the South, predominantly the mountains of northeast Georgia, but also encompassing North Carolina, Tennessee, Virginia, and Pennsylvania.

The majority of us belong to—or are associated with—a group of rug hookers who call themselves "The Happy Hookers of Rabun County." Naomi Stopher, a retired employee with the Federal Drug Enforcement Administration, began the group in 1976, soon after moving to this heavily forested, mountainous area close to the North Carolina and South Carolina borders. Besides its popularity with tourists and retirees, the county's main claims to fame are cabbage and

underwear: it is purportedly the "capital of the world" for both products.

So you see that we are nothing fancy—though we like to think our fiber craft is. Nor are we or our art unique: in communities throughout the country and Canada are similar groups—often similarly named—who relish creating their lush tapestries and primitive rugs. They are a social group: rug hooking does not take the concentration of weaving, though we share its love of texture and color. And rug hookers are extraordinarily friendly and supportive. Why this is so, I do not know, but Atlanta hooking teacher and artist Pat Tritt has her own theory: "You can't have an attitude when you frequent thrift shops," she says, referring to the sites that most hookers haunt to keep their rug supplies flourishing.

The women drawn to this esoteric, almost forgotten craft come from widely varied needlework backgrounds. For some, rug hooking is the zenith of a long needlework career. They had been knitters, crocheters, needlepointers, quilters, weavers, or seamstresses—or all of these. Yet other women become artisans of this craft who have literally never picked up a needle before. And, as these photographs of their rugs attest, all of the rugs turn out beautifully, regardless. All these women are fiber artists.

This "forgiving" quality of rug hooking is, to me, unique among the fiber arts. A crudely knit sweater that is oddly proportioned doesn't fit and is relegated to the back of the closet, and eventually, the wastebasket. A poorly executed needlepoint pillow is unattractive and, mysteriously, turns trapezoidal. But an out-of-proportion drawing on a rug is just more primitive, and thus endearing. And an unexpected color choice just makes you smile. In short, you have to really screw up for even a maiden adventure in rug hooking not to look charming on an old pine floor.

I don't know why this is so, but I have witnessed it over and over again. Many of us confess that our first rugs, mistakes and all, are still our favorites. Perhaps it's because the colors are so rich, the patterns so wonderfully old-fashioned, the fabrics so luscious, that wherever you are or aren't as a fiber artist, rug hooking will make you look better.

There is another quality about rug hooking that may be unique: you can start it right away.

If your enthusiasm for knitting ever faded with the fifth swatch to check your gauge…if you ever cut out 2,000 pieces of calico before beginning a double-wedding-ring quilt, then I need not say more. Put simply, if you want to hook, not build patience, you can buy a pattern and start hooking. (Well, you will need some lessons, but every fiber art takes instruction.)

Yet, and here is another endearing quality of this art, if you want more challenge, there are many more levels to rug hooking than just hooking. You can become a colorist, for example, and dye your own wools. Or, you can create your own patterns. It is this depth of the rug-hooking experience that I think explains why so many women get hooked on this art and never move on (or retreat to) other arts. Rug hooking is just never boring.

Getting Started

If you know already that you're hooked, where do you start? If you can get away for a long weekend or a week, the ideal introduction is a workshop or rug camp. *Rug Hooking* magazine lists all workshops and camps throughout the country, according to geographic region. A camp is a retreat, an artists' colony, and sisterhood (with a few brothers thrown in) all rolled into one. Each camp or workshop runs a makeshift supply store where you can buy your supplies (otherwise, you'll probably need to use mail order suppliers, unless you're lucky enough to have a store nearby.) Your teacher usually dyes your wools and "color plans" your rug. She'll teach you the basics, fill your head with color theory and practical tips, and have you hooking up a storm by week's end.

But a rug camp may be impractical or impossible. Or simply something you may like to treat yourself to once in a while. And you want to hook right *now*. Then what? The next best bet is to locate a rug-hooking teacher in your area. An appendix section lists several sources of teachers. Also, quilters, quilt shops, and quilt conventions sometimes have such information, as more and more quilters foray into what is seen as a companion art for the fiber lover.

Teachers usually have supplies and patterns or will order them for you. As I said earlier, you can begin hooking immediately, though, of course, practice makes perfect.

Or, you can teach yourself. This is often a necessity, depending upon your location. That's fine, too. Many hookers I have met have taught themselves with success. Or you may just want to try the techniques out. If so, here is a list of the most basic supplies.

The Basic Supplies

- **A commercial pattern.** Or a piece of high-quality (Scottish) burlap, linen or monk's cloth on which you have drawn, with a permanent marker, a design. Leave at least 6 inches of fabric all the way around your design to have plenty of room to fit it into a frame.
- **A hook.** These are crochet hooks, mounted in wood. Finely pointed ones are used for tapestry and "fine cuts;" larger-numbered hooks or special primitive ones are for the wide-cuts. But choosing a hook is, in fact, never this simple. There are hooks for the right- and left-handed and for those suffering from arthritis, ones with straight shanks or bent shanks. There are pencil-shaped ones and bulbous-shaped ones. My teacher, Naomi Stopher, used only one hook her whole hooking career, regardless of the cut of her wool: a black ebony one with a fine point. Hooks are personal. (One of the fun things about camp is getting to see and experiment with a wide variety to find the one that just fits your hand.)
- **Wool.** Hookers use 100% wool or, rarely, a blend with not less than 70% wool. You do not want to use too loose a weave: it will ravel and fall apart. You'll need a minimum of 5 times as much wool as the space you are covering. Thus, a 1-foot square chair seat pad requires 5 square feet of wool. Fortunately, hooking wool usually comes in 54-inch widths. Thrift shops are a good source of wool. Be sure to wash and

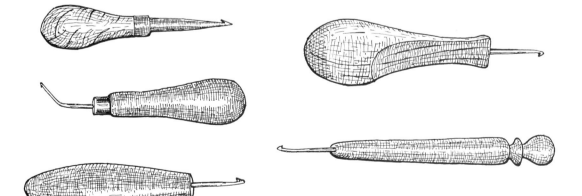

Five examples of rug hooks. Top left and bottom left ones are for primitive hooking. The other three are for smaller or tapestry cuts. The one on the top right with the carved-out section on the shank is for a person with arthritis.

Specially mounted lap hoops, such as this Hasty™ design, are popular with hookers.

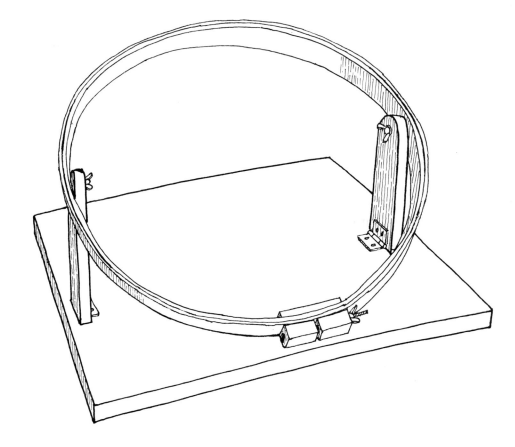

Several varieties of frames are an alternative to wooden hoops. This collapsible plastic one is called a Pittsburgh™ frame.

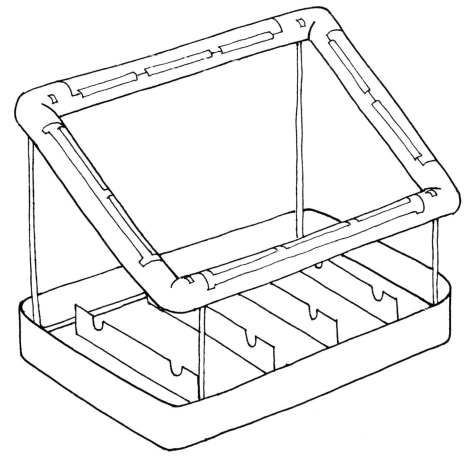

The Art of Rug Hooking

dry the wool so you don't introduce moths into your house and, more importantly, your rug. This process of washing and drying also tightens the weave.

- **A hoop or frame.** A quilter's 14-inch hoop works fine, although most hookers prefer one mounted on a stand. Others use a frame, especially created for hooking. I even know one hooker, in her eighties, who has never used either: she stretches the burlap across her lap and sits on the excess fabric. Her technique and rugs are beautiful.
- **A scissors.**
- **A cutter** (optional, but not for long). A cutter is a machine designed to cut strips of wool. When you feed a strip of wool into one end of the cutter and crank the handle, fettucini-like strips emerge out the other end. The cutter's wheels can be changed so that you can vary the width of your strip of wool from threadlike (a size 2, which you might use for an eyelash, for example) to 3/8 inch (a size 9, good for fur). Fine cut, tapestry hooking usually uses a 3, 4 or 5 cut. Primitive uses bigger cuts: 6–9. (The numbers refer to the width of the strip in 32nds of an inch. Thus, a size 3 cut is 3/32 inch; a size 8 is 8/32 inch, or 1/4 inch wide.) While you are deciding whether or not to invest seriously in this art, you can hand-cut your wool. In fact, many rug hookers always do.

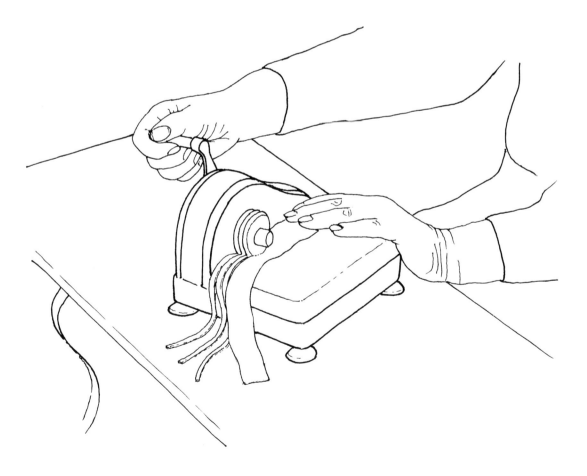

Wool cutters make light work of creating the wool strips needed for hooking. This portable Bliss model is made by Harry M. Fraser Co.

Hand cutting your wool adds texture and an old-fashioned feel to your rugs, as in this one, *Birds in a Bower*,
hooked by Virginia Godfrey, designed by Marion Ham.

Virginia's Godfrey's hand cutting, combined with her unexpected color choices, makes her rugs distinctive.
Pattern: *Wilton Rose Heroic*, designed by Lib Callaway.

"Don't worry about your talent or capability; that will grow as you practice. Katagiri Roshi said, 'Capability is like a water table below the surface of the earth.' No one owns it, but you can tap it."

Natalie Goldberg
Writing Down the Bones

The Basic Technique of Hooking

The best method of learning to hook that I have seen is to mount a piece of screen (the newer, nylon, flexible ones would be gentlest on your fingertips) into a hoop until the screen is taut. This allows you to see what your hand below the rug is doing. This also makes it easier to follow the diagrams and photographs.

Step 1. At a point in the middle of the screen (or fabric), insert your hook, open side down. Hold your wool strip in your other (usually left) hand and poise it to the left of the hook.

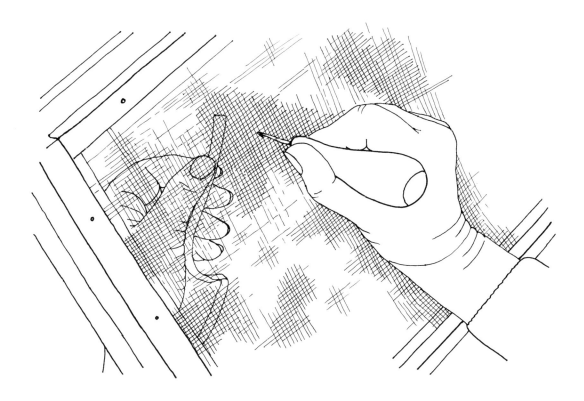

STEP 1: Insert your hook, open side down, into your fabric. Hold your wool strip in your other (usually left) hand and poise it to the left of the hook.

STEP 2A: With the hook, catch the wool from behind, creating a loop. Pull this loop through your fabric.

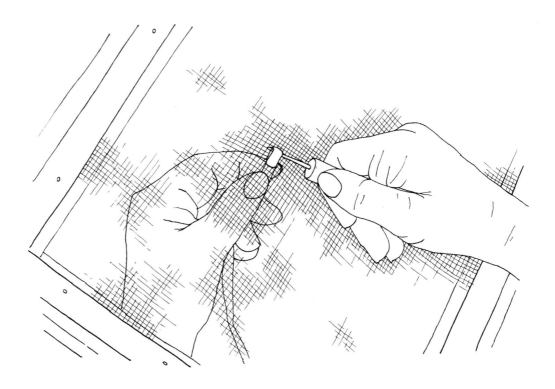

STEP 2B: Close-up of a tail. You have a tail at the beginning and end of every strip. Later, you trim these off.

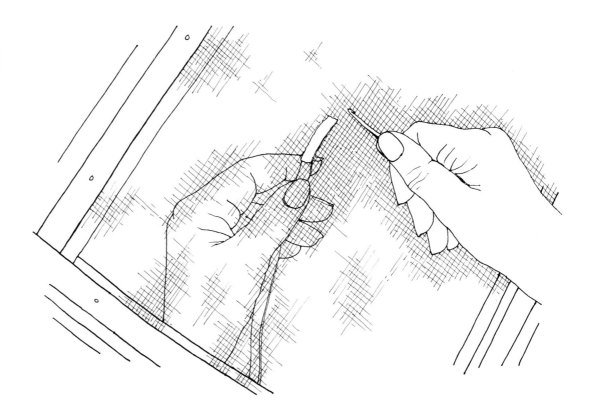

The Art of Rug Hooking

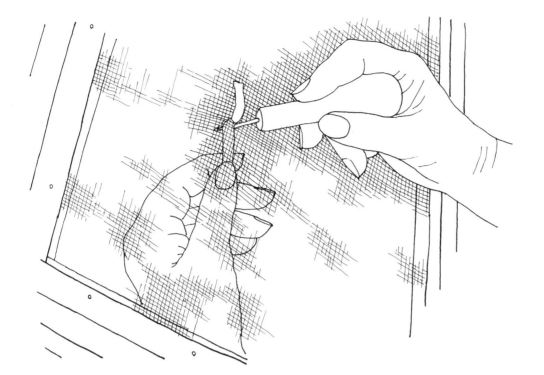

Step 3a: Reinsert the now empty hook to the left of the tail, in the first available hole. Again, hold the wool strip with your left hand.

Step 2. With the hook, catch the wool from behind, creating a loop. Pull this loop through the screen. This is your "tail." You'll have a tail at the beginning and ending of each strip of wool. Always have your tails end on top (i.e., the good side, facing you). Later, you will clip them off. Having the tails on top secures the stitches. It also increases the life of your rug, as any lumps on the bottom side of the rug will become wear spots.

Step 3. Reinsert the now empty hook to the left of the tail, in the first available hole. Hooking is usually done from right to left. Again hold the wool strip with your left hand, poised to the left of the hook.

Step 3b: Close-up of hooking technique.

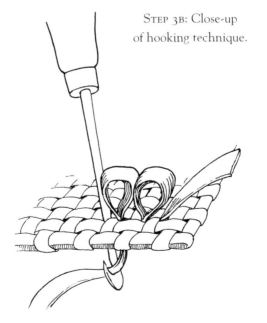

Step 2c: Close-up of hooking and tails.

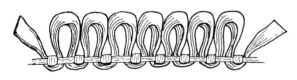

STEP 4: Again, catch the wool with your hook, but this time pull up the entire loop through the hole in your fabric. Pull the loop up to a height approximately equal to the strip's width.

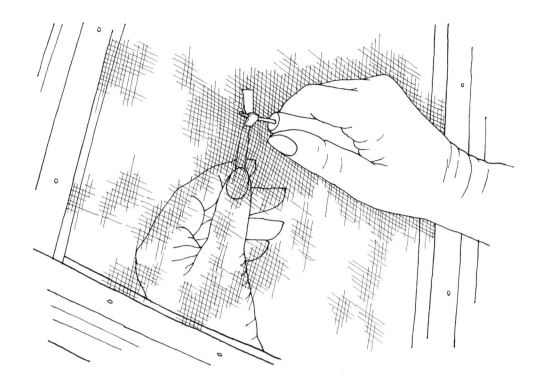

STEP 5: Reinsert the empty hook through the fabric to the left of the first loop. Again, pull the loop up through the fabric to a height equal to the last stitch.

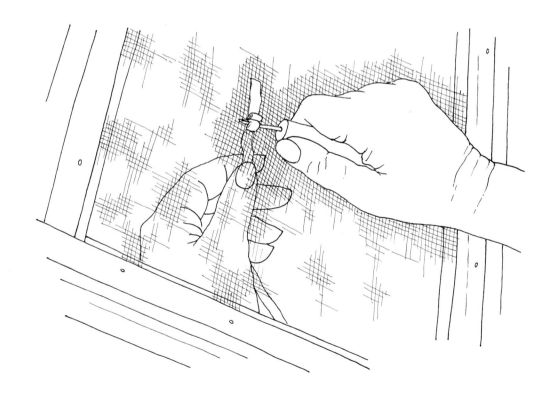

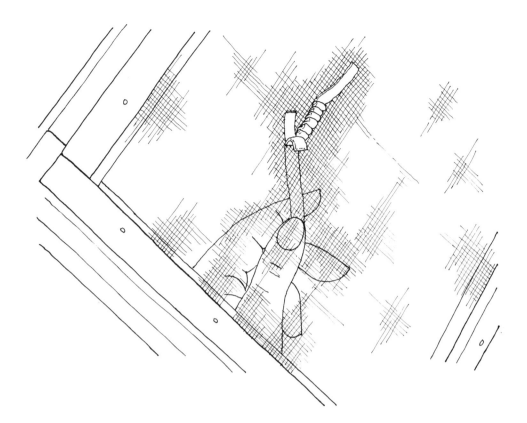

STEP 6: Continue creating loops until your strip ends. Pull the tail up through the top. Pull the tail from your next piece of wool up through the same hole as the ending tail of your last strip of wool.

Step 4. Again, catch the wool with your hook, but this time pull up the entire loop through the hole in your fabric. Pull the loop up to a height approximately equal to the strip's width. Thus, an 8-cut is 1/4-inch wide, so your loop, if you are using 8-cut wool, should be about 1/4-inch high.

Step 5. Reinsert the again empty hook through the screen to the left of the first loop. Exactly where, varies. If you are using very fine cut, you will insert it into the next hole. On a large cut, such as an 8, you will insert the hook into about every other hole. Placing the stitches too close together is called packing and will cause your rug to

buckle. It will also decrease the life of your rug. You do *not* cover every hole in the background fabric, though from the top, the rug gives this appearance. Again, pull the loop up through the screen to a height equal to the last stitch.

Step 6. Continue creating loops until your strip ends. Pull the tail up through the top. Pull the tail from your next piece of wool up through the same hole as the ending tail of your last strip of wool.

Step 7. Repeat this process of creating loops outlined in steps 3–6 until you have covered the area of your rug that you want to be that color.

Congratulations. You have just hooked. This is the basic stitch in hooking and you have learned it.

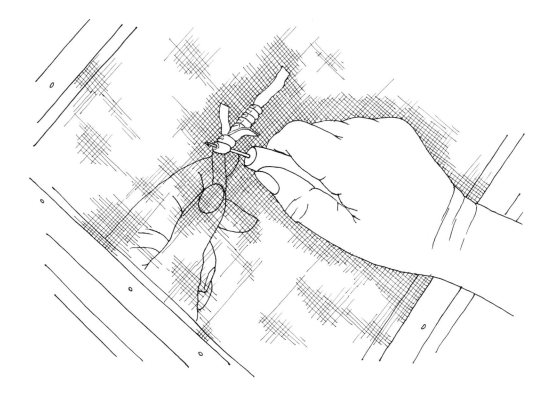

STEP 7: Repeat this process of creating loops outlined in steps 3–6 until you have covered the area of your rug that you want of one color.

Preparing Your Fabric for Hooking

Once you have mastered the basic stitch, you can begin a rug or smaller project. A few projects—including a tote bag and hanging or table mat—are included in this book, with detailed instructions, and other patterns are supplied.

There are three steps to preparing your fabric: obtaining the pattern, stitching or taping the raw edges, and applying binding tape (unless you plan to overcast the edges, which is done when hooking is completed).

The simplest—and fastest—method of obtaining the pattern is to buy one, available from a wide range of designers. Designers often publish modestly priced catalogs, some with photographs of finished rugs, and will mail you a pattern on your choice of background fabric (primitive or regular burlap, linen, or monk's cloth).

The cheapest method is to create your own pattern, by drawing it on your background fabric. Most hookers draw their design first on a large piece of paper, then transfer it to red-dot (an interfacing-like material with red dots every square inch), and only then, finally, to the burlap, linen or monk's cloth, using a felt-tip, permanent marker. When you follow this method, your red-dot will be a permanent pattern for you, should you wish to create a second one.

If you are copying an established design, you can enlarge it using an over-

"It is a formidable camaraderie I've seen
among older women;
I do look forward to that."

Elizabeth Berg
The Pull of the Moon

head projector. Most libraries, even small ones, loan out such projectors. Again, trace the design onto paper, then red-dot, then your actual fabric.

A third method, much more laborious, is to superimpose a grid (i.e., graph paper) on your design. First, determine how much larger you want your final pattern to be. Then mark off a piece of paper with larger grids, and hand-copy each grid, enlarged, onto the paper. I remember having to do this for a display in the third grade, so it's do-able and not that hard. But it is time-consuming. An overhead works better.

But while we're on the subject, copying established designers' patterns from their catalogs is illegal and really frowned upon. Once you get to know the rug designers—and you will, since many of them teach at rug camps— you'll see how hard they work for their money. If you should copy one of their patterns, you can't ever sell the rug or even display it in a rug show, because you have plagiarized the design. So it's just not worth it.

Some common sources of pattern ideas are children's drawings; photos of pets, houses, or favorite objects; and folk art and illustrations whose copyrights have expired. And, of course, you can create your own design. Borders can be altered from existing patterns or copied from clip-art booklets (uncopy-

righted designs). Books of such free-use art and patterns are published and widely available at bookstores.

After transferring a pattern (or buying one), you should zig-zag around the outside edges of the fabric to deter fraying. Or, you can tape the edges down with wide masking tape.

Finally, you should apply your binding (twill) tape next to the outside border of the actual pattern. This tape, about $1^1/2$ inches wide, is available in several colors from hooking supply stores. Choose a color that blends with your border. Buy enough tape to go around the perimeter of your rug, plus about one-third extra. Wash the tape in very hot water until it quits bleeding. (This step is not absolutely necessary; but if you intend to display your rug on top of a carpet and it should ever get wet, the dye from the tape could ruin your rug and carpet.) You can iron the tape dry.

Then, place the tape along the outside edge of your rug. The bulk of the tape will actually be covering up your rug design. Stitch as close as you can to the edge of the pattern and the tape—about $1/16$ inch. Later, you will fold it back, leaving about $1/4$ inch showing. This prevents the tape from pulling at the last row of stitches, which creates an unsightly gap. After applying the tape, do a row or two of zig-zag stitches in the first $1/4$

Rug-hooking teacher Mary Williamson's springer spaniel Ginger greets students with—what else?—wool. This became the inspiration for Mary to adapt Patsy Becker's pattern, *Spaniel*, into a pillow. Note the plaid background, created by carefully cutting and hooking buffalo plaid strips in sequence.

The Art of Rug Hooking

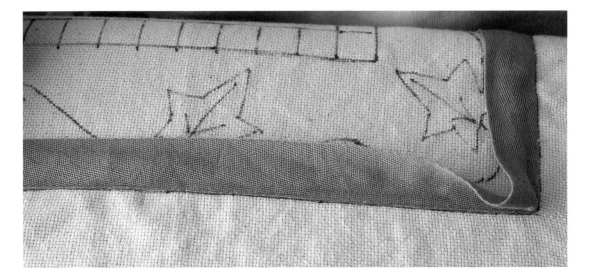

Placing the tape along the outside edge of your rug, stitch as close as you can to the pattern edge, securing the tape.

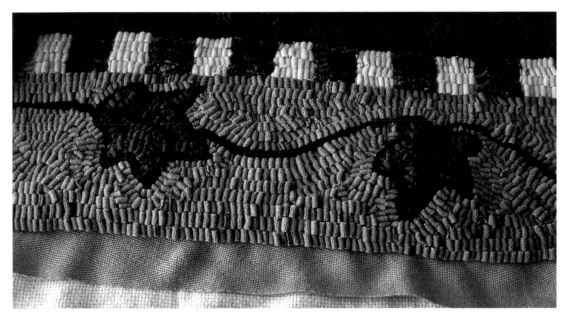

To hook, fold back the tape and hook right up to it. (Leave one thread unhooked to ease tension.)

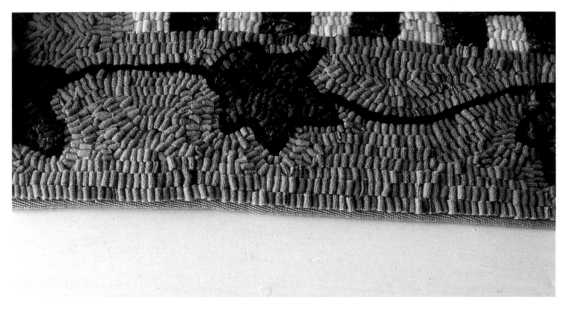

When you have finished hooking, fold the tape and fix to back, but leave about 1/4 inch showing. This will not be visible on the floor but will prevent the tape's pulling at the last row of stitches, creating an unsightly gap.

inch outside the pattern. Later, you will be cutting off your excess fabric, and this will prevent it from unraveling.

You can also add the tape when you have finished hooking. But if you wait, you will have to hand sew it on. If there's anything I hate more than having to take a bunch of steps before I start a project, it's having to do a bunch of ticky things at the end, when I'm anxious to see it finished. So I always put my tape on first.

General Rug Hooking Do's and Don'ts

You have mastered (or learned) the basic stitch, you have your equipment and pattern. You're ready to hook. Where do you start?

Not by cutting tons of wool. This is a beginner's mistake. Cut as you go, or a strip (3^1/$_2$ by 18 inches) at a time. Then you won't end up with a lot of cut wool that you never use.

Begin hooking in the middle of your rug. Choose one object, for example, a flower on the *Mini Ramona* rug project. Outline a flower petal. The outer line is always done *inside* the line, so that your wool touches the line. If you always do this with every line, your design will turn out as you intended. If you are inconsistent with this rule, your objects will be out of proportion to each other. After outlining, fill in.

To fill in your design, hook round and round from the outside to the center. An exception would be a flower; here, you would do the outline, then the center,

One basic rule of hooking is to outline an object before hooking it. This outline is always done just inside the line, so that your wool touches the line.

The Art of Rug Hooking

After outlining, fill in your design, hooking round and round from the outside to the center. Or, with a flower, do the center, then fill in between the center and outline. After hooking an item in your design, always do one or two rows of background around it.

then fill in between. After hooking an item, say a flower or leaf, always do one or two rows of background around it. This will make your design "pop" and straighten out wiggly lines. It will also ensure you have chosen the right background color and get you started on hooking the background, which can be tedious.

To hook background, you usually mark off (with a permanent marker) and hook gentle curves that more or less follow the lines of nearby designs. Then fill them in. However, some hookers almost always hook straight across. Examples of the latter technique are Maryon Clonts' *Thoroughbred* and the sky in *Three Marans*. You can also mix techniques, making the sky swirling but the grass straight across. There are no rules about this.

There are rules, more or less, about how close to make your rows. The rule is: close enough not to leave gaps on top, but far enough apart that ribbons of background material do show on the back of the rug. The background of Mary Williamson's *Endearing Elegance* illustrates this. Beginning rug hookers usually err on the side of putting stitches too close together. This will shorten the life of your rug, use up more wool, and not give the pliable, springy feel you are after.

One exception to hooking from the inside of your rug toward the outside is this: put a holding line around your border. This will help to keep its shape. If you wait until you get there to hook those lines, the border may no longer be straight.

One popular technique for hooking backgrounds is to hook gentle curves that more or less mimic the lines of nearby designs, as in this rendition of Patsy Becker's *Kit's Treasure*, hooked by Virginia Godfrey.

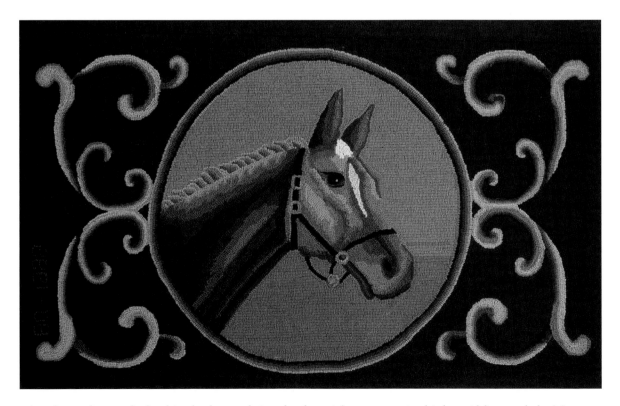

Another technique for hooking backgrounds is to hook straight across, as in this beautiful example by Maryon Clonts. Pattern: *Thoroughbred* by KarlKraft.

The Art of Rug Hooking

Finishing Your Rug

When you complete your rug, carefully cut off the excess fabric around the pattern, leaving about 3/8 inch. Then turn the pre-sewn-on rug tape under the rug, leaving about 1/4 inch showing. (It will not show when hung on the wall or laid on the floor.) This prevents the tape's pulling at the final row and causing an unsightly gap. Pin and hand stitch the tape down.

Then block your rug. You do this by putting the rug, right side against a surface. Put a damp towel on the back side of the rug, then iron it through the wet towel. Let the rug dry before moving it. Dry cleaners will also block rugs for a nominal fee.

An alternative method of finishing a rug is to overcast the edges with needlepoint wool. This is the preferred method of finishing tapestry rugs.

These are the general principles of hooking. Refer to the reminder list of do's and don'ts on page 71 as an aid while you're still experimenting.

Displaying Your Rugs

The most time-honored way to display your rug is on a floor—wood, linoleum, or carpet. Although hookers love to say that rugs last for three generations

Some of your burlap or background fabric should be visible on the back side of your rug. This gives the rug a springy feel and allows the wool to breathe.

Grandma's hand-hooked, hand-designed rug, *The Pink Rose of Georgia*, warms grandchildren's feet on cool mornings in the north Georgia mountains. Artist: Patricia Tritt.

Rugs and quilts seem to go together, as in this guest bedroom in the author's home. Rugs are all hung with carpet tack strips.

of constant use, most of us don't tempt fate: we put them in less-traveled areas of our house, not at the front door. A bed is another popular place: drape it at the bottom, as you would an afghan or quilt.

Hanging rugs is another popular alternative. Depending upon the size of your project, you can attach loops of rug tape on the back and then slide a dowel through the loops. You can also create a sleeve across the back for a dowel.

My favorite way to hang rugs is to use carpet tack strips. These are 4-foot-long narrow strips of wood with two sets of nails already inserted at regular intervals. One set of nails goes into the wall; the other protrudes outward at an angle. Carpenters use these strips around the perimeter of a room in order to hook on and stretch wall-to-wall carpeting. A 4-foot strip sells for less than $1. Have your local carpet supply store cut the strip to about $1/4$ inch less than the length of your rug. Then nail the strip onto the wall, with the outer nails protruding upward, and gently slip the rug tape on the top of your rug onto the small nails.

Beautiful hooked pieces become a focal point in decorating, as in this assortment by Patricia Tritt. Large rug is *Flat Flowers*, designed by Lib Callaway.

OBTAINING WOOLS

It doesn't take an Einstein to realize that if every rug takes five times its surface area in wool, you will need a lot of material if you're going to become a hooker. Here are some sources of wools.

Thrift Shops

If your heart starts beating when you spy a new thrift shop sign, you're a born hooker. In fact, some of us have been known to scout out the thrift shops in a new site before the antique shops—a sign of a serious positive addiction. The rows and rows of colorful, varied skirts, vests, slacks and coats are a virtual treasure trove for the fabric artist—and at bargain prices. For rug hookers in warmer climates where woolens are scarce even in fabric stores, field trips to thrift shops are a necessity.

But, you can get burned. Avoid anything with iron-on interfacing; even if you peel it off, it leaves a residue. This means most blazers are out. Also, pass by coats that are made of very thick pile and, conversely, items that are very loosely woven. The former will not hook nicely; the latter will fray.

Try to buy only items that are labeled 100% virgin wool, or in a pinch, for a fabulous fabric, a 70% wool blend. Be careful, though. It's not unusual, after taking apart a straight skirt, to discover you have only 1/2 yard of "as-is" fabric… and that is after washing it and taking apart all the seams. You might find that you can get a medium-priced wool on sale in your area for less money and trouble. Also, as-is materials are, by definition, often used and worn and might have dry-cleaning chemicals on them.

(Though all of us can describe in detail the perfect plaid Pendleton skirt we found with its original store tag on it!)

For the obvious reason that you get much more wool for your money, look for larger sizes: this is one time that a size 16 is best. The best yields are pleated, A-line or full skirts or dresses and shirts. Blazers are rarely worth the trouble of disassembling and often have interfacing. In terms of what types of wools to buy, this is a wonderful chance to stock up on basic solids. Camel-hairs overdye into gorgeous reds. (See the red background of *Mini Ramona*, for example; it is all overdyed plaids and camel-hairs.) Light greys and whites are also great for overdyeing. But be aware that unless the item you are buying is really large, it will probably not yield enough yardage to do, say, an entire background. When combined with other wools, it will take dye differently. A good example of this is seen in my rug, *Three Little Kittens*. The mottled sky in this rug was all white, 100% virgin wool from skirts found in thrift shops. They all looked the same color before dyeing. In this case, this variegated effect is what I wanted; but if you want a solid, flat look, you should buy yardage.

Thrift shops are also a wonderful source of plaids, tweeds, checks and herringbones. Don't just shop for what you need now. You will need a cache of materials not only for your next rugs but for overdyeing. At first you might be disappointed by how many brown and grey tweeds you run across and tend to avoid them. But, as is, these make wonderful bears, cats and tree trunks. Plaids make perfect flower petals, waves, and borders. Like antiques, the time to buy such cheap woolens is when you see them.

Ten Do's and Don'ts of Rug Hooking

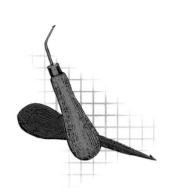

1. Do make sure your burlap, linen, or monk's cloth is taut in your frame. Don't leave your pattern in a hoop overnight or for long periods of time when you're not working on it.

2. For very even stitches, exaggerate your loops, pulling them up an inch or so high. Then, with the hand under your hoop or frame, slowly pull the loop down to the height of the previous hoops.

3. Always hook inside lines on a pattern—not on the line.

4. Early on in your project, put a "holding line" all around the inside of your border. This will ensure that the lines of the border are still straight when you get to them.

5. Begin hooking near the center of your pattern, gradually working your way out. Put outline lines around designs; then fill them in.

6. It's perfectly acceptable to use more than one size cut on one pattern. But when you do, make sure your loops are all the same height.

7. For balance, always have some bright and some dull colors in each rug.

8. If you're not sure that you'll have enough of one color wool, hook several strips with it, but don't trim your tails. Now you can see exactly how far your wool will go. If you even suspect you will run out of a color, try to re-buy or re-dye. If you do the latter, but notice a difference in hues, pull out random strands of the color everywhere you have hooked. Re-hook using the new color. Then mix all of the wool—both dye batches—together and proceed with hooking.

9. As you're working, save all scraps: you might need them. And when you have finished a piece, fill a plastic sandwich or twist-tie bag with swatches of all the wool you used and label it, in case of repairs down the line.

10. To clean your rug, don't vacuum it. Sweep it, underside first, then top-side. For spots, use a commercial spot-cleaner, but check first for colorfastness.

"Boring" beige and grey tweeds and plaids can make a gorgeous tree trunk, as in this example from a work in progress by Judy Hill.

Finally, it's worth your while to contact your area's thrift shops and learn when they have their "bag sales," when you can buy all that you can stuff into a bag for a couple of dollars, usually at season's end. Mark these on your calendar. In our area, the hookers make a day of it, on such occasions, going from shop to shop and ending with lunch.

Local Teachers

These are your best source of good, dyed wool. And many teachers now also sell as-is material that has been cleaned and disassembled at a fraction of the price of new wool. Prices vary by region of the country and are always escalating. But, generally, new wool costs $2^{1/2}$ times the cost of as-is. Overdyed new, premium virgin wool, made just for hookers and braiders (Dorr wool), will sell for 4 to 5 times as much. Virtually every rug teacher sells Dorr wool, and many of the favorite formulas for leaves and flowers and backgrounds stipulate a Dorr wool (say celery green) overdyed with certain colors (such as khaki).

Some people use only Dorr wool and only new wool, arguing that for all the work and time they are investing in their rug the materials should be the best possible. Also, new, high quality wool has a wonderful silken feel and is a delight to hook with. Moreover, there are items that require it—faces, for example, or rugs using a very fine cut. Other hookers, particularly primitive hookers, use only as-is, enjoying the foray into fabric stores almost as much as the dyeing and hooking. They feel the scrounging and the saving links them with their rug-hooking forebears, and they feel very virtuous for recycling.

Many of us just happily nestle in the middle: buying the gorgeous, overdyed blue Dorr that we can't do without for a starry night sky or background, but using plaids and other as-is for grass, trees, and scarecrows. Happily, our rugs seem to enjoy our very American blending of the old and new, becoming all the richer for their variety of textures.

Wool Suppliers and Outlets

There are also numerous suppliers of rug-hooking wools. Some even supply pre-cut #6 wool (called "hookettes") and pre-cut #3 strips ("strippettes"). Many of these suppliers advertise in *Rug Hooking* magazine. If you have fabric outlets in your area, visit them regularly.

Plaids make wonderful waves, as in this Pat Tritt original, *Fourth of July at the Lake*. Santa doll is one of a variety produced by Sweet Briar Studio. Fisherman is an adaptation of a Sweet Briar pattern.

Using variations of a color in your background adds interest and depth to your rug, as in this example of an anything-but-dull black background from a rug hooked by Patricia Tritt. Rug: *Flat Flowers* by Lib Callaway.

USING COLOR

"Rug hooking is all about color," Naomi Stopher, my teacher and the founder of the Happy Hookers of Rabun County, used to say. And it's true. Marjorie Judson, the great rug-hooking teacher who lives in Prince Edward Island, tells her students that the first thing your eyes go to is color, then composition. Last is technique.

So, if you've never had an art class, where do you start? Here are a few tips that will launch you into this wonderful world of color.

Color Plan Your Rugs

As a general rule, plan out your rug's colors before you begin hooking. If you don't, you will find yourself constantly switching colors to find what matches what you have already hooked. Nomie always used to say that the background should be chosen first. Actually, what usually happens is that you fall absolutely in love with a piece of fabric and it inspires a whole rug. But Nomie's point is well taken; early on, decide on your background color because it touches everything, which means it affects all the other colors in your rug. The one rug I did not do this on, I ended up trying four different backgrounds. It was an awful experience of "reverse hooking" (a hooker's euphemism for ripping out).

Some rules-of-thumb on backgrounds. Grey rarely works: it deadens the other colors; avoid it. Black, on the other hand, "crisps up" other colors, so it always is a popular background. To get interest in your background, especially if you have a lot of it, you can collect many plaids and solids and "marry them," or steep them together in hot water until they blend together, using either dye or a teaspoon of detergent without bleach. Then you do not have a solid look, and your background has "movement" to it. This is illustrated in Pat Tritt's background in the rug opposite and in Judy Hill's rendition of Marion Ham's *Plantation Fruits*. In both of these rugs, the background is so vibrant and rich. What's more, a variety of wools—rather than one solid color—is more interesting to hook. The one thing you don't want your background to do is detract or compete with the details in the rug. Like a frame, it should enhance subtly.

A good starting point for color planning is to put your pattern on the floor or table and start placing wools that appeal to you where you think they'd go. You will quickly see that colors change in relation to each other and that the lovely blue looks garish next to that red, and that the poppy red suddenly looks orange next to a certain green. This is all trial and error. When you think you've got a good mix, stand way back or blur your eyes. Does any color jump out at you? If so, expunge it. Try something more subtle.

Have and Use a Color Wheel

Way back in elementary school you learned that the primary colors are red, yellow and blue, and that their complements are the colors formed by blending two of the primaries. If I have already lost you, then forget color theory for the moment and just look at this color wheel made from dyed wool. Find a color. Trace your finger across to the exact opposite on the wheel: that is the complement of your first color. If you are

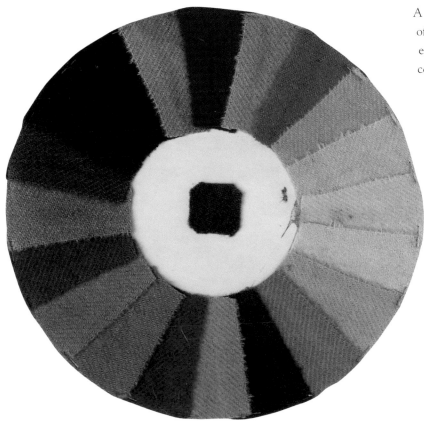

A color wheel, made of dyed wools, is an excellent guide for color planning and dyeing wools.

In her original pillow design, *The Flower Basket*, artist Patricia Tritt uses a dozen different colors in the basket alone.

The birds and flowers in this rug get their vibrancy from assorted tweeds, plaids, and solids. Rug: *Cornell Garden*, hooked by Patricia Tritt, designed by Marion Ham.

The Art of Rug Hooking

trying to color plan, and you need another color but are stuck, get out your wheel and find the complement of one of your colors. It is always a good choice. So green, for example, looks good with red; lavender with yellow.

The color wheel also comes in handy with dyeing. The way to dull a color is not always to add black, but rather to add the color's complement. Thus, if your red is just not deep enough, you find your red on the color wheel, find the complementary green, and add a little of that to your dye bath.

Beginning dyers often have a lot of fabrics turn out a muddy color. This happens when you use equal parts of complementary colors in a dye bath: it always produces mud.

Repeat a Color Three Times

I've heard this called the triangle theory. You rarely use a color just once in a rug because that will make your eye gravitate to it. This is especially true with whites and yellows (which can mysteriously look like fried eggs plopped in the middle of your rug), but it really applies to all colors. Also, don't lump your use of one color in just one area of your rug. Jeanette Szatkowski's lovely rug *Mini Ramona* is a good illustration of the balance that happens when a color is repeated three times in various areas of your rug.

Use Many Variations or Hues of a Color

Obviously, if you just use a Dutch blue in three places on a rug, a recida green three times, and an Egyptian red three

times, the rug is going to be boring. Here is where you play with texture—tweeds, plaids, checks—and color (spot dyes, for example). Depicted opposite are two originals by Atlanta artist and rug hooking teacher Pat Tritt, whose forte is color. Note how many browns she employed in *The Flower Basket,* how many colors and textures she used in the birds and the petals of Marion Ham's *Cornell Garden.* This rich use of color is the art of rug hooking.

Trust Your Instincts

The first rug I ever sold, I sold because I didn't feel it was "me." I had had an artist renowned for her color sense as my teacher, and I realized early on that it would be a battle to assert my own sense of color. I knew she was a master, and I wanted to learn from her, so I made the decision to surrender to her sense of color during this creation process. I did learn a lot, and the rug was absolutely gorgeous. But I was never comfortable with it—or rather, it was never comfortable in my home. It didn't fit, and I don't mean that the colors didn't match. It just did not express me; it stood out. So I sold it and now it happily graces someone else's cabin.

At class, I have often heard a teacher say, when asked about a color choice, "Well, it isn't a color I'd pick, but if you love it, use it. This is your rug." I agree with this. Rug hooking is an art, so it must express your own creativity, not your teacher's. Go with what you love and learn to work with it. If you make mistakes (and you probably will), you will learn from them, which, after all, is what mistakes are for.

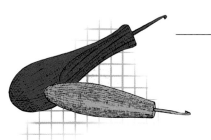

*"As a child, I always loved to color.
And rug hooking reminds me of coloring."*

Marguerite Culberson

LEARNING TO DYE

The final color tip is a big one: learn to dye. There is no rush here. I hooked for five years before I tried it. But, eventually, as Pat Tritt phrased it, "You have to do your own dyeing if you want to get anywhere."

There are books galore on dyeing. Rather than repeat them here, I am going to give an overview of the basic dye process, information on some dyeing terms, show you the results of different techniques, and list a few basic resources. Some of these are old, hand-distributed pamphlets by well-known hooking teachers; they are inexpensive, no-frills, and distributed wherever dyes and supplies are sold. *Rug Hooking* magazine has a column on color by the incomparable color genius Maryanne Lincoln every month; this primer with that column and these inexpensive resources can get you started.

Dyeing wools is accomplished by soaking them in a steaming dye bath in a large porcelain or stainless steel pot. White enamel is best because you can see the true color. The bath consists of hot water to which a mordant (*un-iodized* salt for chemical dyes; alum, tin, chrome or iron, depending upon the dye, for natural dyes) and a dye have been added. Following are four common dyes used in the United States and Canada:

- **Natural dyes** (made from vegetables, berries, weeds, insects and the like). The snouts and beige border of my *Dancing Bears*, for example, are made from ground chestnuts. Natural dyes give gorgeous colors; however, if you don't use the right mordants, the colors are not fast. Moreover, just because a color is natural does not mean it's not poisonous. Many are. Finally, natural dyes are very surprising. Red cabbage and alum, for example, yield a deep sapphire blue; sassafras roots make pink. The take-home message about natural dyeing is that it's not for beginners. Study up and do it right. One resource: *Dye Plants and Dyeing* by John and Margaret Cannon; Timber Press, Portland, Oregon.
- **Cushing dyes.** Cushing has been manufacturing colorfast dyes for rug hooking for over a century—since 1879. Today's Cushing dyes are called acid dyes and are available in 94 colors. They are expensive, but produce beautiful colors; moreover, many of the beloved, tried-and-true rug-hooking formulas for backgrounds, scrolls, leaves or flowers are based on formulas that use Cushing dyes.
- **Magic Carpet dyes.** Produced in Hamilton, Ontario, these dyes are the most popular ones with Canadian rug hookers.

- **Pro Chem dyes.** These are much newer chemicals, sold in larger amounts but for far less than Cushing dyes. However, they can produce brighter, sometimes garish colors. Colorist Maryanne Lincoln recently developed formulas for the Pro Chem dyes that approximate the rich, subtle colors rug hookers have learned to expect from Cushing dyes. Her collection of such formulas and dyeing hints is available from her or through Pro Chem.

As I mentioned, there are numerous methods of dyeing. I am going to discuss here the basic overdyeing method that I employ, using Cushing dyes, and define several dyeing terms you will encounter. Exact details of dyeing should be obtained from the resources listed or a rug hooking teacher. The accompanying photos illustrate the results with each technique.

Overdyeing

Begin by presoaking the material that you are going to dye in very hot tap water to which have been added a few drops of a wetting agent or detergent. Too much of such products actually takes color out, so use them sparingly.

While the wool is soaking for at least one hour (some purists do it overnight), assemble your materials. They are:
- a large stockpot
- newspapers or old towels to spread on a surface near the stove
- un-iodized salt
- dye spoons (double-ended spoons sized as small as $1/128$ teaspoon to ensure accuracy) or measuring spoons

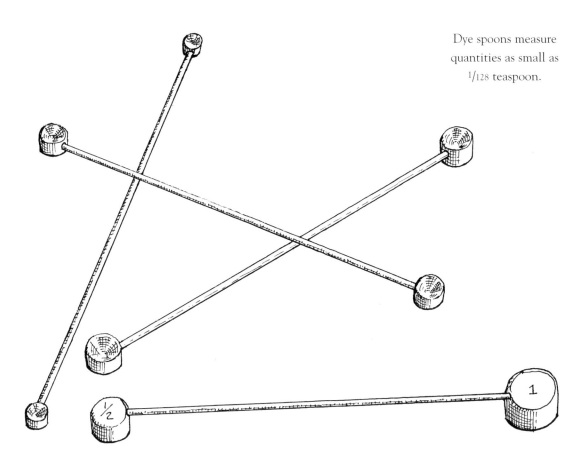

Dye spoons measure quantities as small as $1/128$ teaspoon.

Four overdyed wools. The slight variations in color are considered desirable and are obtained by not stirring the wool much when it's in the dye bath.

- Pyrex measuring cups (at least 3, since many formulas use three dyes)
- dye
- rubber gloves. Bluettes, insulated gloves available from your hardware store, are best.
- wooden spoons
- scissors (to cut wool and open dye packets)
- glass jars for storing leftover mixed dyes
- white vinegar
- a color chart (a sheet that shows you what the colors are supposed to look like) or a formula book.

Then begin the dye bath. Fill a large (soup-stock size) white enamel pot with tap water in which about 1/2 yard (or 7 oz.) of wool can comfortably sit and not be packed. Add one tablespoon of un-iodized salt and begin heating on burner.

In the meantime, prepare a cup of boiling water. Measure the dry dye powder according to the formula you are using and dissolve it in the cup of boiling water. (Stir it for a minute to make sure it's dissolved.) When ready, add the dye solution (in the amount stipulated in the formula you are using) into the pot of heated water. Note: the water should *not* be boiling. Stir well. Then add your wet (*not* wrung-out) wool. Give it a good stir and let it cook for about 30 minutes. Then lift the wool out (using rubber gloves and tongs), add 1/2 to one cup white vinegar, stir well, and re-submerge the wool. After cooking until the water has become almost clear (about 30 more minutes), turn off the pot and let the water sit overnight or until cool. You must cook acid-fast dyes an hour or they're not colorfast. Then rinse your wool well (wearing thick rubber gloves) and transfer it (un-wrung-out) to the washing machine. Put it through the rinse cycle and then either line dry or dry it in a clothes dryer on very low heat.

Leftover dye solutions are stored in labeled glass jars and used within a couple of weeks. The pans and all utensils are cleaned with a bleach solution and stored out of sight—away from kitchen utensils. You never want to accidentally use your dye materials for cooking.

Finally, when the wool is dry, clip a piece and put it, together with the formula used and the date, in a little dye journal. If you need more material later, this will remind you of exactly what you did. The date is important to note too because those of you on water systems (as opposed to wells) may note wide variations in your dye results even though you used the same formulas. This could indicate when chemicals have been added to your water supply. Keeping a calendar can alert you to good or bad times of the month.

That is the basic dyeing process. It is called overdyeing or, simply, dyeing. Four sample overdyed materials are depicted opposite. The variations in color you see on these samples are considered desirable and are accomplished by stirring the wool very little. Conversely, if you want a very uniform color, stir the pot a lot.

Spot Dyeing

Spot dyeing is a process of deliberately introducing spots or blotches into the wool. Remember the tie-dyed T-shirts of hippiedom? Those are good examples of spot dyeing. Spot-dyed materials are a wonderful resource in hooking: they make great autumn leaves, snow shadows, and clouds, to name just a few examples.

The effect is created by crumpling wet wool into a lasagna-sized pan that has been lined with wrinkled aluminum foil. Dissolved dye is spooned, by tablespoons, onto the wool in spots. Several colors of dye can be used. The wool is then salted, and boiling water added along the sides. This concoction is then covered and baked at a low temperature.

Of course, the other half of the spot-dye equation are the formulas you use. When you first get into rug hooking, colors will seem almost like a secret code. You'll ask about a particularly unusual color in a rug and the teacher will respond, "Oh, that's a Dotti Ebi." Or there will be great whispering about Jeanne Benjamin's secret—and wonderful—parchment background formula. One reason that teachers are so valuable to the beginning rug hooker is their familiarity with the many formulas for dyeing. They can thus assure you that you will get the exact colors you want in your rug.

Dotti Ebi—along with Maryanne Lincoln, Claire de Roos and many others—are colorists whose formulas have become famous in the rug-hooking world. Most have published these formulas in inexpensive pamphlets. Dotti Ebi's, for example, is called *Scraps or Spots: 115 Formulas for Rug Hooking*. Two other basic "texts" for spot dyeing are *Prisms #1* by Claire de Roos and Nancy MacLennan, which contains 64 spot formulas and 35 formulas for oriental rugs, and *Prisms #2* (same authors), which contains 159 swatch formulas for rug hookers using wash-fast acid dyes (Pro Chem dyes). These three resources are widely available from hooking suppliers for about $6 each.

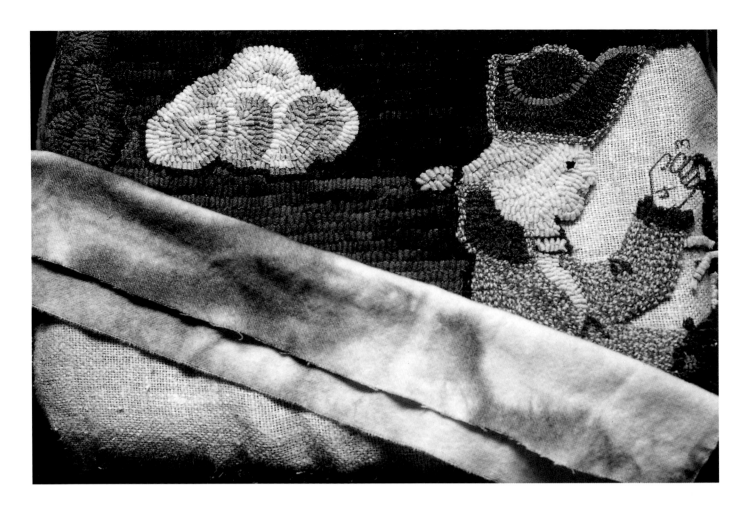

Above: Nancy Mumma's glorious clouds in her rendition of Marion Ham's *Paul Revere's Ride* were made from the spot-dyed wool shown atop it.

Right: Spot dyeing adds variation and shading without changing wools. It is ideal for grass, trees, leaves, and snow, for example.

The Art of Rug Hooking

Dip Dyeing

For this method, you begin with steaming, stove-top water to which dye has been added. First, you drop all of your wool into the dye bath. Then you immediately pull it out and begin dipping it into the dye bath 1/3 or 1/2 way up the swatch until you get the color you like. Some people safety-pin the wool strips to a small coat hanger to do this, which gives the process its other name: coat-hanger dyeing. This type of dyeing, depicted below, is often used for scrolls in traditional hooking.

Dip dyeing is often used for scrolls, or flower petals, such as these by Mary Williamson.

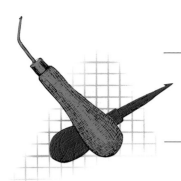

> *"Every rug needs a little poison."*
>
> **Rug-hooking proverb**

Results of
casserole dyeing.

Casserole Dyeing

Like spot dyeing, casserole dyeing employs a large, flat casserole pan. But in this case, you start off with an inch of water to which vinegar has already been added. After cutting wool into large, pan-sized strips, you begin putting in alternate layers of wool and dye solutions. Then cook it in the oven or on a stove top. The results are similar to dip dyeing.

Gradation Dyeing
(jar method)

Tapestry rugs often use different values of the same color—sometimes as many as 16 hues, which might range, for example, from a white-tinged pink to a deep fuchsia. This is what makes a hooked peony look real enough to pick. One method of gradation dyeing that is popular uses 6–8 (or more) wide-mouthed canning jars. As in canning, the jars are arranged in a roasting pan with hot water. From one cup of dye solution, $1/2$ is poured into one jar. Then hot water is added to the cup of dye solution to make it 1 cup again. Then $1/2$ cup of the weakened dye solution is poured into the next jar. The process continues—refilling the dye solution to 1 cup, pouring $1/2$ cup into another jar—until the number of values you want is reached. Extra water and salt are then added to each jar and individual strips simmered in each jar for one hour. The result will be gradations of colored wool.

Gradation swatches such as these were created with the jar method of dyeing.

Painting

For special effects, such as sunsets, some hookers actually paint their wool. With this technique, the wool is first soaked in water to which 1/2 cup of vinegar has been added. A paintbrush is dipped into a dye solution, which also contains vinegar, and the wool is painted by hand. The effect of this technique is shown below.

Hand painting wool creates special effects.

As this brief overview suggests, the world of color and dyeing is rich in possibility. Lessons in dyeing are offered at most rug camps. Indeed, many teachers at camps incorporate dyeing into the lessons. If you start collecting as-is materials now, your teacher can dye for you until you decide to attempt it.

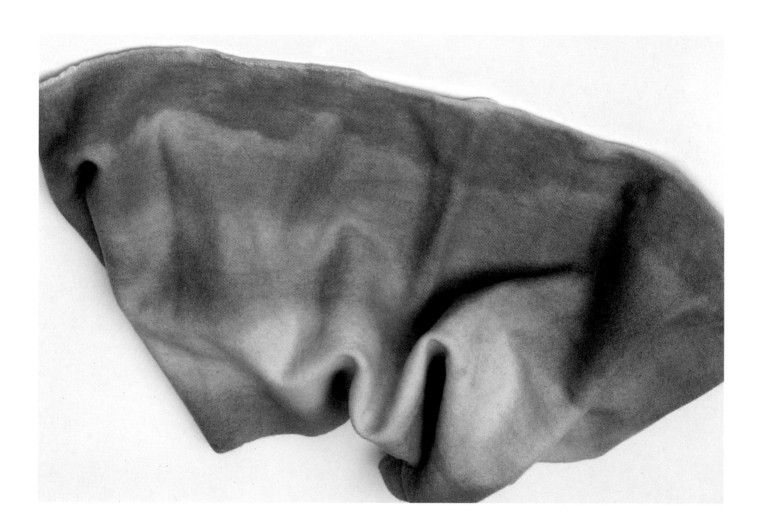

The Art of Rug Hooking

A wall of colorful
wools in Mary
Williamson's hooking
room.

PROJECTS

CLAMSHELL TOTE

Bag Design: Jacque Juvennal
Hooking Pattern: Anne Mather

Clamshells (or lamb's tongues) are as frequent in rug-hooking patterns as they are in quilting. Usually, this pattern is used for borders. But in this design, adapted from an 1800s rug, clamshells constitute the entire design.

This is a fun project because it teaches you about color placement and because you can use scraps and leftovers to create it. I used black for outlining the clamshells and for background, but any dark color will do. Variations of five basic colors—red, gold, green, blue, and lavender—were used on the shells themselves.

This colorful clamshell tote bag uses up leftovers and teaches color placement.

Size

13.5 by 13.5 inches

Materials

Wool fabrics in the following colors and approximate quantities:

- 1 yard black background
- 2¹/4 yards as-is and leftovers in five basic colors: red, gold, green, blue, and lavender
- ¹/2 yard lining (flannel print)
- linen or burlap
- yarn
- 10 inches Velcro

Hooking Instructions

1. Enlarge pattern to 30 inches by 16 inches wide. Transfer to burlap or linen. Monk's cloth is not suitable for this pattern: it's not stiff enough.
2. Zig-zag (or fold masking tape) around perimeter of burlap or linen to keep it from fraying.
3. Using the photograph and fabric list as guides, hook design. Start by outlining in black around the border of the rug and around each clamshell. Then begin experimenting with color. This is a hard piece to "color plan," per se. But you do need to be careful to repeat each color several

Some of the fabrics used to create the clamshell tote bag.

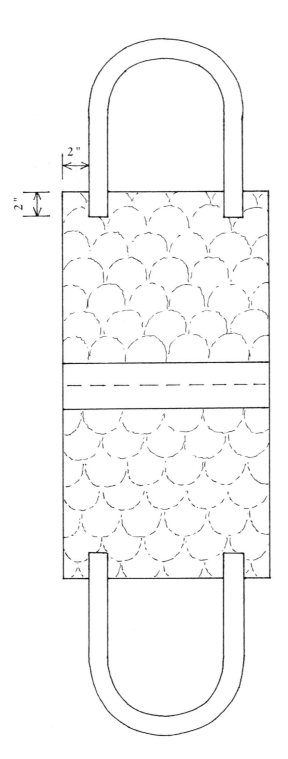

Wrong side of
hooked piece.

2"

2"

Assembling the Tote

1. Use the diagrams as guides.
2. Handles: Make two straps (handles) cut from background wool. Each should measure 34 by 4$1/2$ inches. Turn under and press $1/2$ inch on each side. Then, fold handle in half, lengthwise, and press. Topstitch down the length of each handle about every $1/4$ inch (about 7 times) with a dark thread. Sew straps by hand firmly to the wrong side of hooking at each top end, about 2 inches from the side edges as illustrated here.
3. Lining: Cut lining fabric 4 inches longer and 2 inches wider than hooking (approximately 34 inches by 18 inches). Mark centers at the side and top with a chalk pencil, straight pin, or fabric marker, see sketch at right.
4. Pocket: To make your pocket, cut a 19- by 12-inch piece from the extra lining material. Turn the pocket edges under $1/2$ on all sides and press. Then fold in thirds to create a 6- by 11-inch pocket. Machine stitch pocket onto lining about 5 inches up from the center. Stitch the center of the pocket to the lining, creating two 6- by 5 $1/2$-inch pockets.
5. Closure: Sew two 5-inch strips of Velcro on the center top of lining, about 3 inches from the edge as shown.
6. Assembly:
   a. Sew under and press $1/2$ inch of lining all the way around and then sew it, by hand, to the wrong side of hooking.
   b. With the right sides of hooking together and using wool yarn, sew

times in various places on each side. A surprising variety of wools are used to create this effect.

4. Block.
5. Overcast all sides of bag with matching wool yarn.

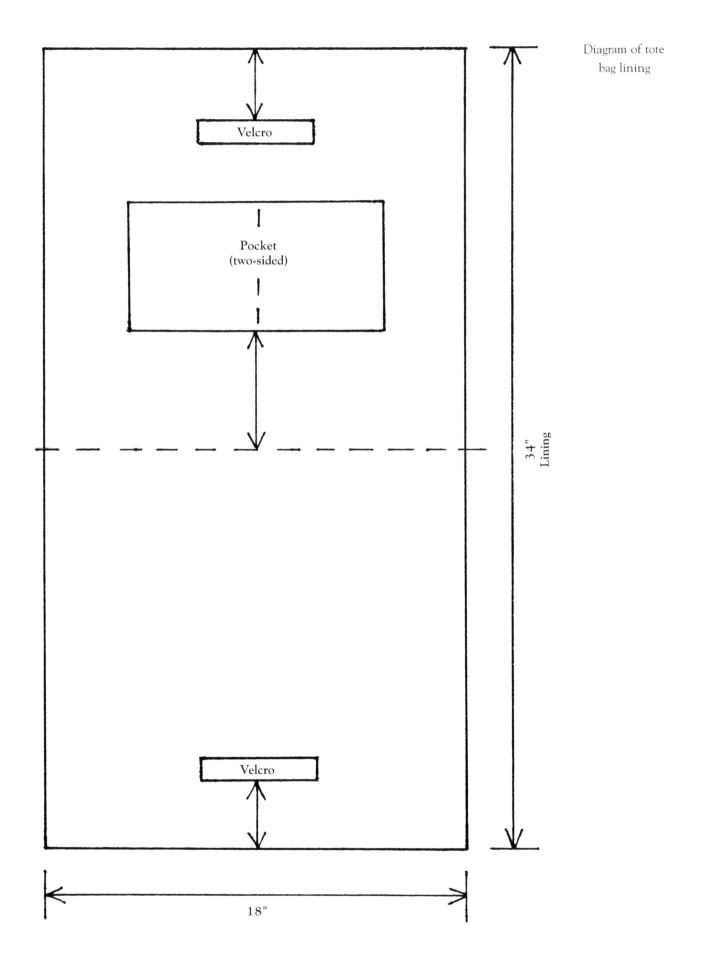

Diagram of tote
bag lining

Velcro

Pocket
(two-sided)

34"
Lining

Velcro

18"

the sides of the bag together into the overcast edges, as you would sew together parts of a hand-knit sweater. Sew the side seams from the top down to 3 inches from the fold. When you have done this on each side, flatten out the bottom to make a 3-inch flat bottom or gusset; it will resemble an inverted "T." Then stitch across the bottom of each "T," attaching the bottom to the sides.

c. Turn the bag right side out. The side gusset should resemble the sketch below. Tack the front and back tops together 1 1/2 inches from each edge to form side gussets and to hold bag in shape.

Close-up of gusset treatment.

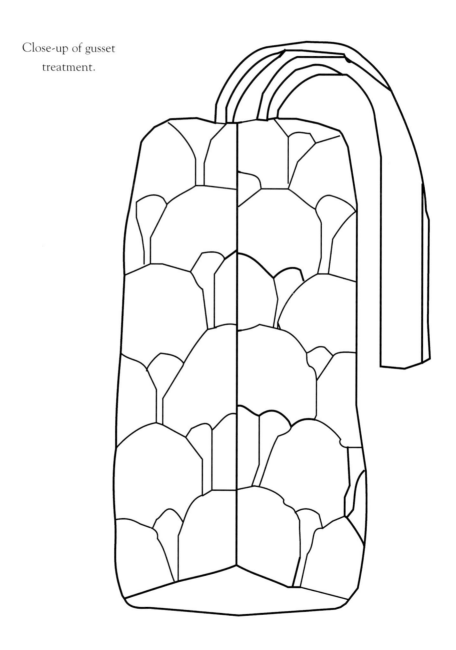

MINI RAMONA

Designed by: Jeanette Szatkowski
Hooked by: Anne Mather

Mini Ramona treats a traditional rug-hooking subject, flowers, in a primitive fashion, using tweeds and plaids. Designed by Jeanette Szatkowski, Harry M. Fraser Co.

Flowers are perennial favorites among rug hookers. In this warm and colorful design, you get to try your hand at a variety of sizes and shapes of flowers and leaves. In hooking this rug, I used a mixture of as-is (herringbones, tweeds and solids) and spot dyes (for leaves and stems). The rich, red background was a variety of woolen tweeds, plaids and camel's hair overdyed together in one pot with Cushing's Egyptian red by Mary Williamson. It's what inspired me to hook this rug. Most of the other dyeing was done by Naomi Stopher. This rug illustrates very well two basic principles of primitive rug hooking. The first is the use of the outline-and-fill technique. Notice how a plaid is used as an outline, and a solid for the filling, or vice versa. Second, the colors in the rug are always repeated at least three times, in various parts of the rug, forming a large triangle. This is a good rug for using up scraps and as-is materials.

Size

23 by 35 inches

Materials

Wool fabrics in the following colors and approximate quantities:

- 1 yard red background
- 1/4 yard bright green spot-dyed wool
- 1/8 yard olive green spot-dyed wool
- 1/8 yard brown-green spot-dyed wool
- 1/4 yard bottle-green and blue-green solids (veins & leaf outlines)
- 1/4 yard medium green tweed or solid (smaller leaves)

- 1/2 yard assorted light, medium and dark-blue tweeds and solids
- 1/8 yard lavender tweed
- 1/8 yard purple (mixture of tweeds and solids, darker for outline)
- 3/16 yard assorted light, medium, and dark gold solids (six 3- by 18-inch strips)
- 1/8 yard gold tweeds
- one 3- by 18-inch strip orange
- 3/16 yard brown (six 3- by 18-inch strips)
- one 3- by 18-inch strip black-and-white herringbone
- 33 by 45 inches burlap, linen or monk's cloth
- 4 1/2 yards masking tape (optional)
- 3 1/2 yards rug-binding tape

Instructions

1. Fold masking tape around perimeter of fabric to keep from fraying.
2. Transfer the design to the fabric.
3. Zig-zag twice at $1/4$ inch and $1/2$ inch from outer border of rug.
4. Apply rug tape.
5. Using the photograph and fabric list as guides, hook designs. Start with large flowers in the middle, hooking the outlines of leaves and centers first, then filling in. Do background as you go along, following the shapes of the nearby leaves and flowers. Plan your varieties of greens for leaves so that they form color triangles.
6. Be sure to hook in your initials and the date you completed the rug.
7. Fold over tape to back; pin; and sew in place.
8. Block by hand or at dry cleaners.

DANCING BEARS HANGING

Hooked and design adaptation
by Anne Mather

This very popular design is actually based on a painting by William Beard entitled "The Bear Dance." These whimsical, pot-bellied, dance-'til-they-drop bears make a delightful rug, wall hanging or table mat. You could also just hook two or four bears for a smaller design, say for use with the tote bag pattern. I used as-is tweeds for the bears; plaids for the grass; and spot-dye for the leaves, trunk and background. All dyeing was done by Mary Williamson.

Size

15 by 33 inches

Materials

Wool (60-inch) fabrics in the following colors and approximate quantities:

- ¹/₂ yard soft-yellow for background and "whites" of eyes (Cushing's old

Dancing Bears uses overdyed tweeds to give the effect of fur, and simple shading lines to create movement of the bears and shadows in the grass. Hooked and adapted, with permission, by Anne Mather from GEAR's wallpaper design, American Country wallpaper book, Imperial Wallcoverings.

ivory, ecru and champagne over Dorr natural wool)

- 3/8 yard dark-brown tweed for bears
- two 3- by 18-inch strips light brown tweed for contrast fur
- three 3- by 18-inch strips beige for snouts and one row of border
- 3/16 yard (six 3- by 18-inch strips) black for outlines
- 1/4 yard green plaid for grass and tree shadows
- 1/8 yard green spot-dyed wool for leaves
- one 3- by 18-inch strip rust spot-dyed wool for tree trunks
- 1/4 yard rust-red for border
- 25 by 43 inches burlap, linen or monk's cloth
- 4 yards masking tape (optional)
- 3 yards rug-binding tape

Instructions

1. Fold masking tape around perimeter of fabric to keep from fraying, or zig-zag.
2. Transfer the design to the fabric.
3. Zig-zag twice at 1/4 inch and 1/2 inch from outer border of rug.
4. Apply rug tape.
5. Using the photograph and fabric list as guides, hook designs, using an 8 cut except for bear outlines and features (snouts, eyes, which use a 5 cut). Start with two bears in center. Begin by outlining bears in the 5-cut black then fill in with 8-cut brown tweed, using lighter shades of the same tweed to indicate areas closer to you, such as bellies and forearms. Eyes are a circle of 5-cut stitches; black center is pulled up after the circle is hooked. Snouts are 1 or 2 rows of 6-cut beige. After hooking the two center bears, hook the center tree, surrounding grass and background, using an 8 cut. Then put in border "holding line" of red; this holds your rectangular shape. Continuing outward from the center, hook bears, grass and background, ending with border.
6. Be sure to hook in your initials and date you completed the rug.
7. Fold over tape to back; pin; and sew in place.
8. Block by hand or at dry cleaners.

$\mathcal{P}$ATTERNS

Antique Fruit Basket. Designer: Lib Callaway (Martha Morris); pattern now owned and distributed by Margaret Siano.
Size: 25 by 35 inches

The Art of Rug Hooking

Blue Ridge Rug Camp. Designers: Robin Hasty and Jeanette Szatkowski (from drawing by Deborah Maghill Bradshaw).
Size: 22 by 29.5 inches

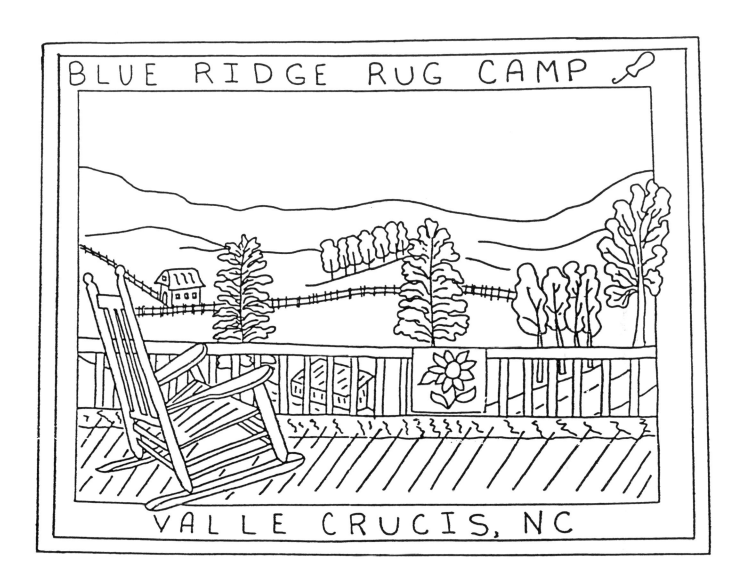

Endearing Elegance. Designer: Pris Buttler (adaptation). Size: 29 by 32.5 inches

the ENDEARING ELEGANCE of FEMALE FRIENDSHIP

FRIS BUTTLER © 1997

Lakeside Cabin. Designer: Kathy Morton, Morton House Primitives. Size: 20 by 30 inches

Rose Bird. Designer: Patsy Becker. Size: 24 by 34 inches

The Art of Rug Hooking

Woman Who Ran with the Wolf. Designer: Anne Mather. Size: 26 by 30 inches

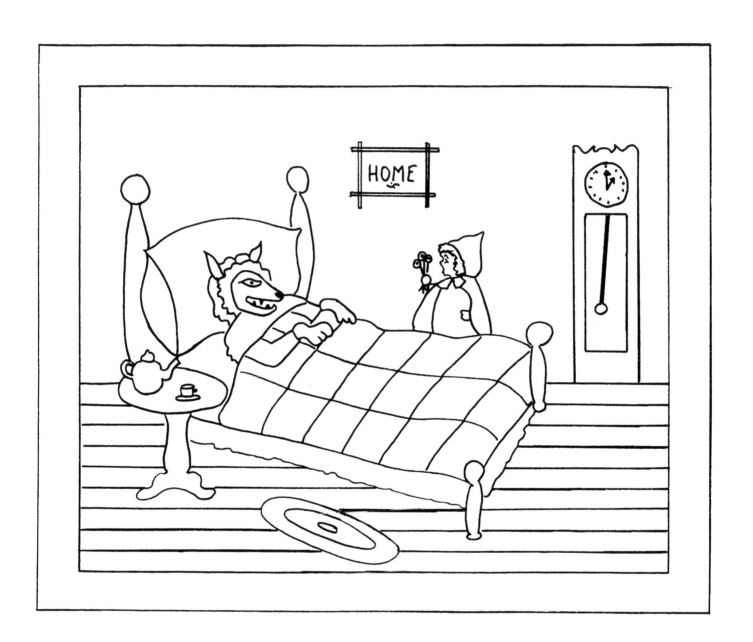

$\mathscr{A}$PPENDIX

About the Hookers...

Pris Buttler is a folk artist, whose primitive paintings have appeared on magazine covers and greeting cards and hang in numerous private and corporate collections, including Georgia Governor Zell Miller's. She lives with her family in Gainesville, Georgia. *You Can't Have My Wool Sweater* is her first hooked rug.

Maryon Clonts is a retired university math professor and the former "Number Lady," who taught elementary math on public television in Tennessee. She now divides her time between her homes in Andersonville, Tennessee, and Dade City, Florida. She has one son and two wonderful stepchildren and enjoys hooking rugs for her grandchildren.

Mary Lu Cole, raised in Michigan, is a retired Air Force Lieutenant Colonel, who served as a psychiatric nurse. She lives in the mountains, in Rabun Gap, Georgia.

Marguerite Culberson is an artist and homemaker, living in Lawrenceville, Georgia, with her husband, Rick, and two children, Matthew and McKenzie. *Two Houses Welcome* is her first hooked rug.

Edith Gerver is an accredited McGown teacher and award-winning hooker who resides in North Carolina but will soon be moving to Washington, D.C. She teaches at several workshops and rug camps. Her second love is raising and showing Maine Coon cats.

Virginia Godfrey was born in Savannah, Georgia, but later moved to Atlanta, where she and her husband raised their three children. She retired to the North Georgia mountains in 1990.

"I used to feel so guilty that I wanted time for me. But I got over that."

Mary Williamson

Beverly Goodrich lives with her husband, Garth, on Lake Lanier in Gainesville, Georgia. She has three grown daughters and one granddaughter. She has been hooking for five years. Her love of boating and Nantucket Island is reflected in some of her rugs—all of which she designs. She is also a woodcarver and folk art painter. Her hand-carved angels and Santas have been featured in such national magazines as *Victorian Christmas* and *Country Accents*.

Bryan Hancock started hooking in 1982, after admiring old hooked rugs that she couldn't afford. She lives in Rocky Mount, North Carolina, on a horse farm. She and her husband, Mike, and daughters, Catherine and Rebekah, live in a log home, which is a great setting for her hooked rugs.

Judy Hill is a homemaker, antiques dealer, and mother, who lives with her husband, Mark, in Highlands, North Carolina. She has a son, Peter, and two grandchildren.

Faith Kern is a full-time farming wife with a background in art. She began "painting with wool," as her first teacher termed hooking, in 1980. For the first seven years, she hooked tapestry-style rugs but now really enjoys wide-cuts. She especially enjoys the freedom primitives give, using recycled wool, and overdyeing plaids and checks. Together with Jane King, a well-known hooking teacher, Faith holds rug-hooking retreats at Lakeside Lodge in Star, North Carolina.

Anne Mather is the author of several books as well as an editor for the Centers for Disease Control and Prevention. She wrote *Just for Today* (Harper San Francisco) and was co-author, with Louise Weldon, of *The Cat at the Door and Other Stories to Live By* (Hazelden, 1991) and its sequel, *The Cats in the Classroom* (1995). She lives with her husband, Brian Kelly, and their two children, Maggie and Jeannie, in the mountains in Rabun Gap, Georgia.

Bett McLean attended The Memphis College of Art in the early seventies. For the next 19 years she worked in graphic design, for a time as art director, for a publisher and a national media company. She is a recent convert to rug hooking. She designs all of her rugs, enjoying this new use of her design skills and knowledge of color. She lives with her 6-year-old daughter, Hannah, and husband, Doug Renfro, in Knoxville, Tennessee.

Barbara Moran is a retired Air Force Lieutenant Colonel; she served as an air evacuation nurse and counselor. A transplanted Rhode Islander, she lives in the north Georgia mountains.

Betty Morning was a McGown-certified rug hooking teacher, who delighted students from 1975 until her death in 1998.

Martha Morris, a mother of three children and grandmother of four, lives in Gainesville, Georgia, with her husband of 54 years, William T. Morris, Jr. She has won national and international awards for her miniature portraits on ivory and recently an award for her newly published book on genealogy. Rug hooking has been her favorite hobby since 1968.

Kathleen Russell is a native Pennsylvanian, who has been hooking rugs since 1974. A McGown-certified hooker, she taught traditional rug hooking and hand-dyeing techniques for years. She has also taught art in the public schools. Her rugs and hangings have been exhibited at Old Sturbridge Village, Massachusetts; The Hershey Museum of American Life; and the Women in the Arts Exhibits at the William Penn Memorial Museum in Harrisburg, among other museums and galleries. Kathy and her husband reside on a farm in Carlisle, Pennsylvania. Both are therapists in private practice. They have two grown children. *Soul Melody,* the rug featured here, was a national winner in A Celebration of Hooked Rugs III (1993), an annual contest sponsored by *Rug Hooking* magazine.

Naomi Stopher was a former administrative officer with the Federal Drug Enforcement Administration, in work that had her living in such places as Brazil and Thailand. When she and her husband, Charlie, retired in the mountains in Clayton, Georgia, in 1976, she learned rug hooking. Soon thereafter, she started the Happy Hookers of Rabun County, a group of three dozen or more rug artists whom she taught this craft. Maryon Clonts, Mary Lu Cole, Marguerite Culberson, Virginia Godfrey, Judy Hill, Barbara Moran, Anne Mather, and Mary Williamson were among her students. Naomi died in July 1997 at the age of 79. She taught her weekly rug-hooking class the day before her death.

Patricia Tritt is an artist who turned her creative talents to rug hooking 10 years ago. She designs most of her rugs and is a rug-hooking teacher. She and her husband Bob have lived in Georgia for 35 years. They now divide their time between Atlanta and Lake Rabun (Lakemont, Georgia).

Mary Williamson is a retired dressmaker, sewing teacher, and mother of three. A McGown-certified teacher, she teaches in several rug camps annually, including Blue Ridge (N.C.), Cedar Lakes (W. Va.), Caraway (N.C.), and Lazy Hills (Tex.). Her work is in many private collections. She lives with her husband, Carey, in Clayton, Georgia. When Naomi Stopher died, Mary opened her home to the Happy Hookers of Rabun County and continued the tradition of teaching the local women to rug hook.

TEACHERS

Need to locate a rug-hooking teacher in your area? Here are some excellent starting points. And chances are they'll be as happy to hear from you as you are to hear about them.

National Guild of Pearl K. McGown Rug Hookrafters, Incorporated
289 George Arden Avenue
Warwick, RI 02886-4860

Will give you names of rug hooking teachers in your area.

Association of Traditional Hooking Artists (ATHA)
Judy Long, Editor, Newsletter
3209 Erwin Drive
Plano, Texas 75074

ATHA maintains a directory of hookers in the United States.

Rug Hooking
500 Vaughn St.
Harrisburg, PA 17110-2220
(800) 233-9055 to subscribe.

This excellent resource magazine for hookers has a column of teachers in each issue, as well as geographic listings of workshops and rug camps, and advertisements for pattern designers and suppliers of a wealth of rug-hooking materials, including woolens. The magazine also publishes a Sourcebook, a definitive listing of teachers, hookers, guilds, and suppliers.

The Internet

The Rug Hooker's Network:
http://www.rughookersnetwork.com)

Acknowledgments

I am deeply grateful to Ted Slautterback, creative writing teacher extraordinaire, who encouraged me to write about rug hooking; to all of the Happy Hookers of Rabun County and elsewhere who contributed rugs, ideas and support for this book; to Ron Lindahn for our many photographic sessions; to Tom Mather for his painstaking sketches; to Jacque Juvenal for creating the tote bag design and to Paulette Carpenter for sewing the bag together and testing the directions; to the following designers, who donated patterns: Patsy Becker, Pris Buttler, Robin Hasty, Kathy Morton (Morton House Primitives), Margaret Siano (Lib Callaway Patterns), and Jeannette Szatkowski (Harry M. Fraser Co.); to my Sterling editor Claire Bazinet for her thoroughness and grace under pressure; to my writers' group, who've been lavishly encouraging; and to my family.

GLOSSARY

Acid dyes - colorfast dyes for rug hooking.

As-is - used wool, especially plaids, checks, and tweeds, often obtained from clothing in thrift shops. As-is fabrics are frequently used in primitive rug hooking.

Backing - the material on which rugs are hooked. The three most popular fabrics are burlap, linen and monk's cloth.

Blocking - steam ironing a rug to shape it and even out the stitches.

Casserole dyeing - dyeing that uses a large, flat casserole pan, which is placed in an oven or on a stove top. The results are similar to those with dip dyeing.

Color chart - a one-page sheet from a dye manufacturer that shows you what color each dye should produce.

Color planning - determining which colors to use for every part of a rug, from background to border to designs.

Cutter - a machine (usually hand-cranked) designed to cut strips of wool for rug hooking or braiding.

Dip dyeing - a type of dyeing in which wool strips are dipped into a dye bath until the desired color is obtained. Dip-dyed strips often have several colors on one strip.

Dye bath - steaming water to which a mordant and dye have been added; used for dyeing wools.

Fine-cut - a description of hooking that uses fine ($3/32$- or $4/32$-wide) strips of wool.

Gradation dyeing - a type of dyeing used to obtain many different values of the same color.

Marry - to steep wools together to make them bleed into one another.

Monk's cloth - a heavy, cotton fabric in a basket weave used as backing for rugs.

Mordant - a chemical that fixes a die.

Overdyeing - dyeing over an already-colored fabric to create richer or different tones.

Pictorial - a rug that depicts a scene or picture.

Primitive - a rug hooked in wide ($^6/_{32}$-, $^8/_{32}$-, $^9/_{32}$- or hand-cut) strips, using an outline-and-fill method, little shading, and traditional subjects (flowers, animals) drawn in a naive style.

Red-dot - an interfacing type material, with red dots every square inch, used to create and trace patterns for hooking. Marker ink goes through the red-dot onto the backing material, transferring the pattern.

Reverse hooking - ripping wool strips out of a hooked area.

Rug camp - a school for rug hookers. Usually held at a campsite, college, or vacation site, each school has several teachers, who specialize in different types of hooking. Students sign up in advance for a specific teacher and work intensely with her for a period ranging from 3 days to a week. Camps are held in every area of the United States, in other countries around the world, and even aboard cruise ships.

Spot dyeing - a process of dyeing in which spots or blotches are deliberately introduced into the wool. Resembles tie-dyeing.

Tapestry - rug hooking that employs finely cut (size $^3/_{32}$- or $^4/_{32}$-cut) strips of wool and detailed shading.

Whipping - overcasting the edges of a tapestry rug with wool yarn.

Wide-cut - rug hooking with large ($^8/_{32}$-, $^9/_{32}$-, or hand-cut) strips of wool. Usually, but not always, such rugs are also primitives.

$\mathcal{I}$NDEX